I Have Two Hearts

To Benny and Elizabeth,
whose love and understanding made this possible

I Have Two Hearts

by
Janice
Schwegler

PRICE/STERN/SLOAN
Publishers, Inc., Los Angeles

I have two hearts that beat as one.
I feel them beating when I run.

My hearts are pumps that push my blood
all through my body, doing good.

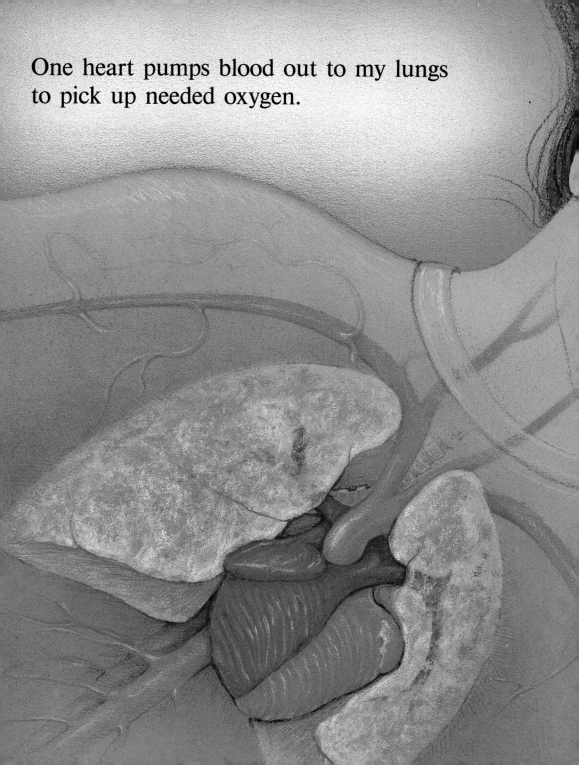

One heart pumps blood out to my lungs to pick up needed oxygen.

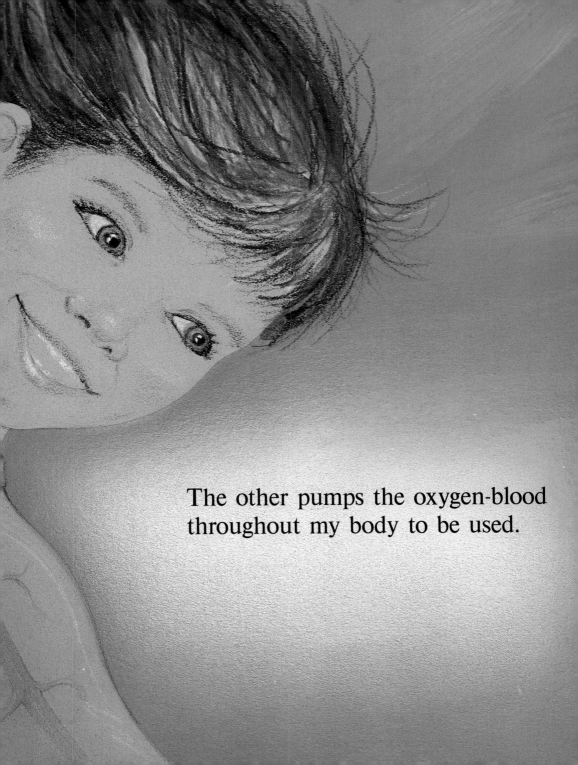

The other pumps the oxygen-blood
throughout my body to be used.

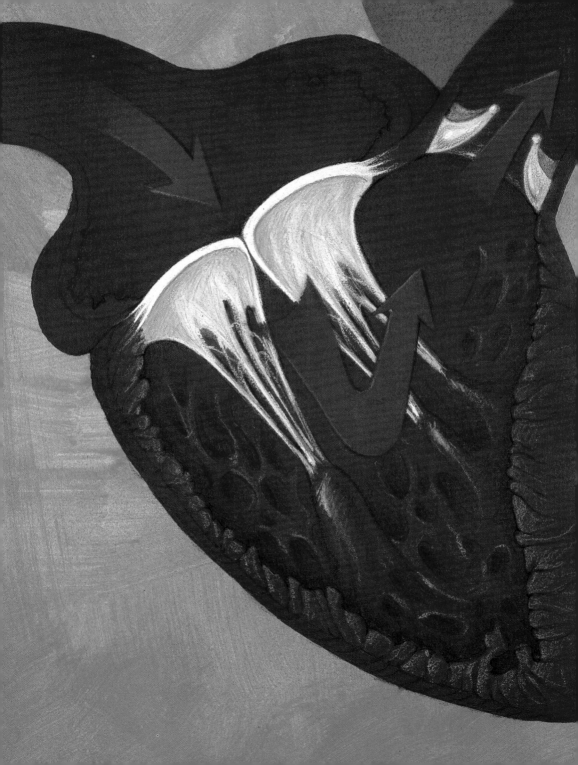

The blood first fills
   my heart at right.
To keep it in,
   a valve shuts tight.

The muscle walls
   squeeze and contract.
A new valve lets the blood
   rush out.

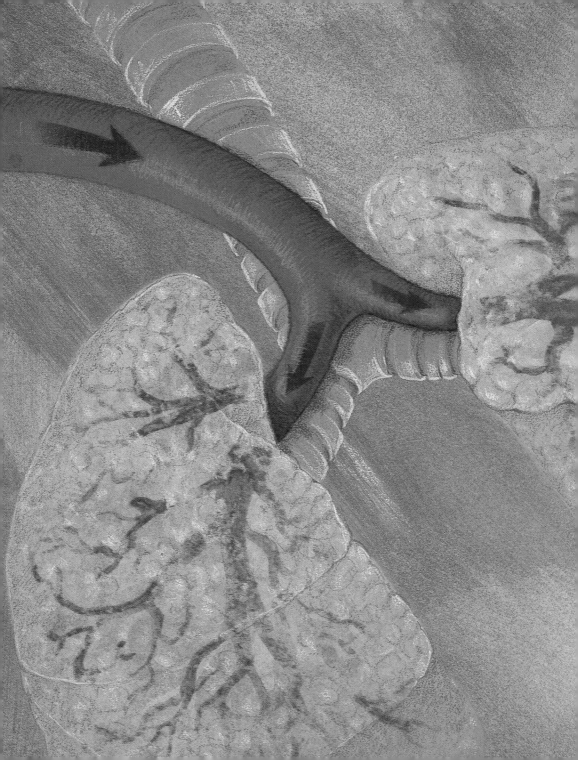

My blood flows out with force so strong,
into arteries and out to my lungs.

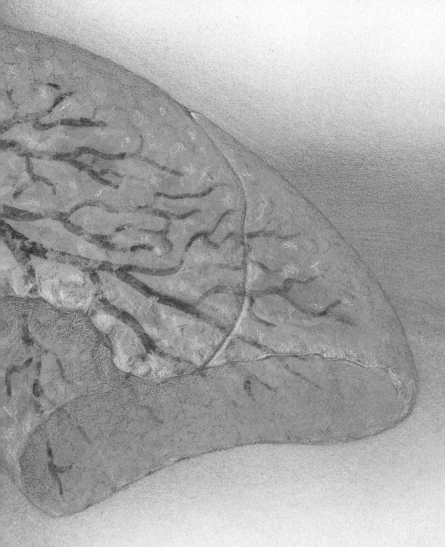

These branching pipes are filled with blood
to make a net of tiny tubes.

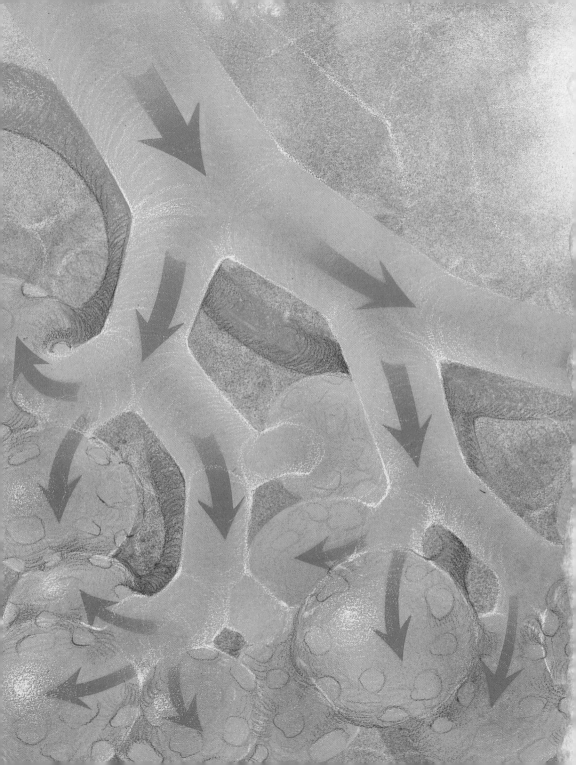

My lungs are made very like a sponge—
a million tiny air balloons.

When I breathe in, the sacs all fill
with airy elements I need.

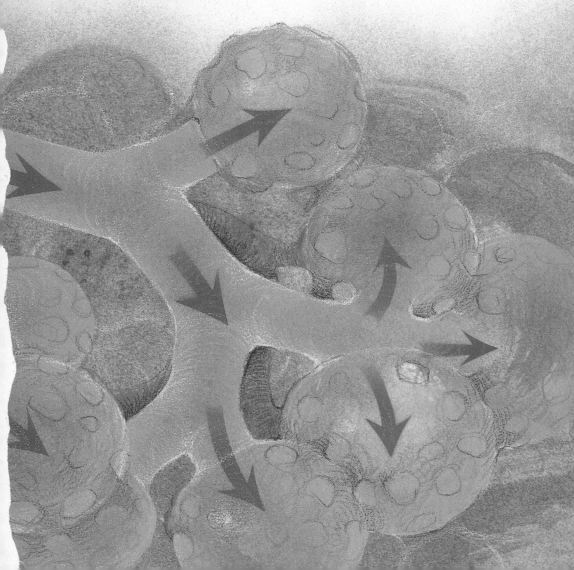

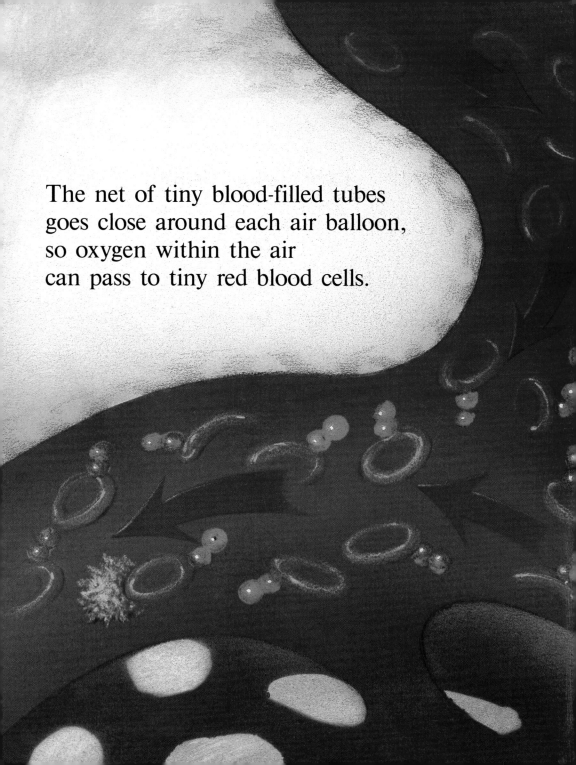

The net of tiny blood-filled tubes
goes close around each air balloon,
so oxygen within the air
can pass to tiny red blood cells.

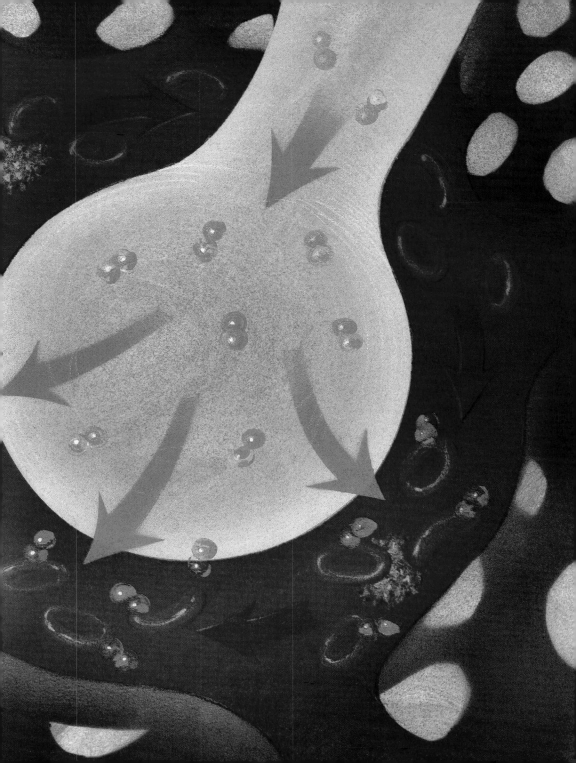

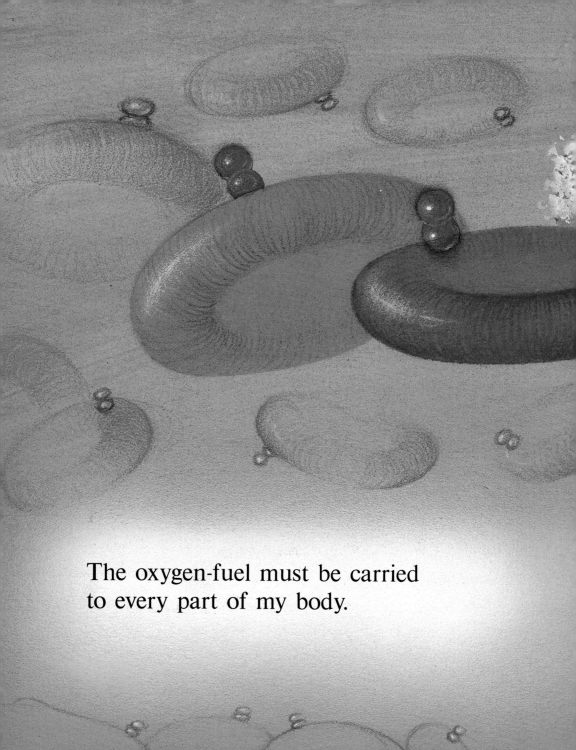

The oxygen-fuel must be carried
to every part of my body.

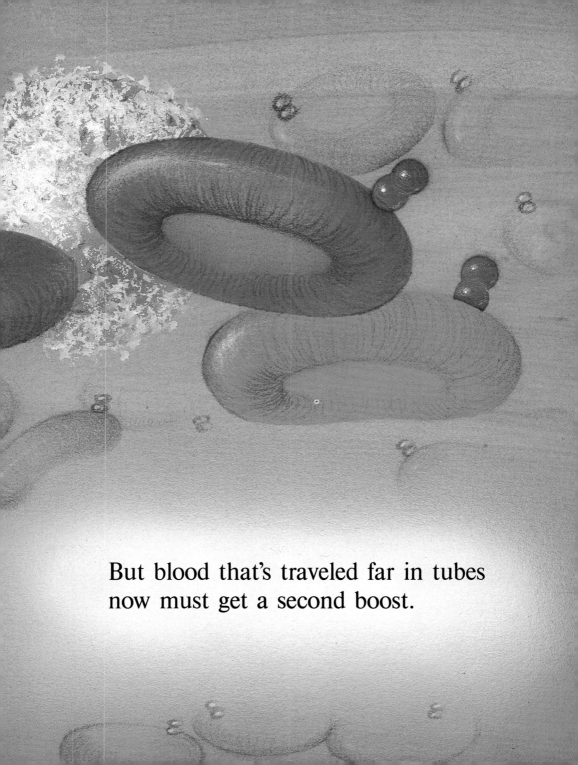

But blood that's traveled far in tubes
now must get a second boost.

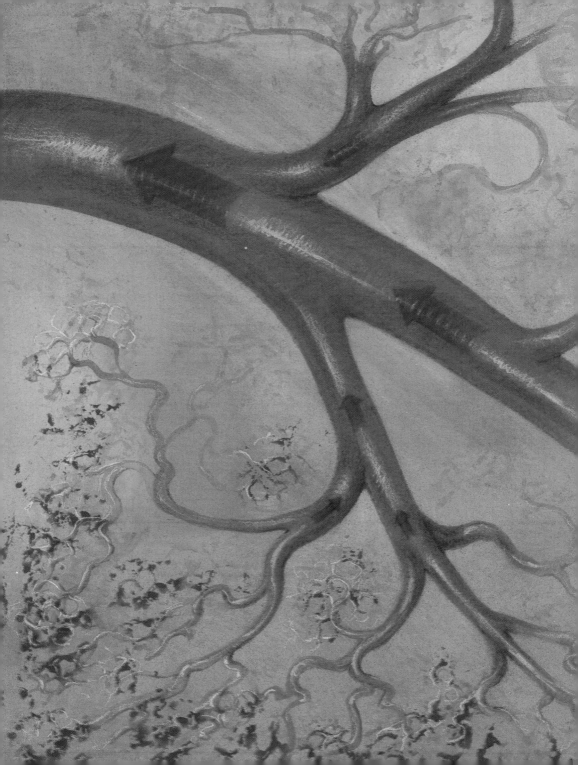

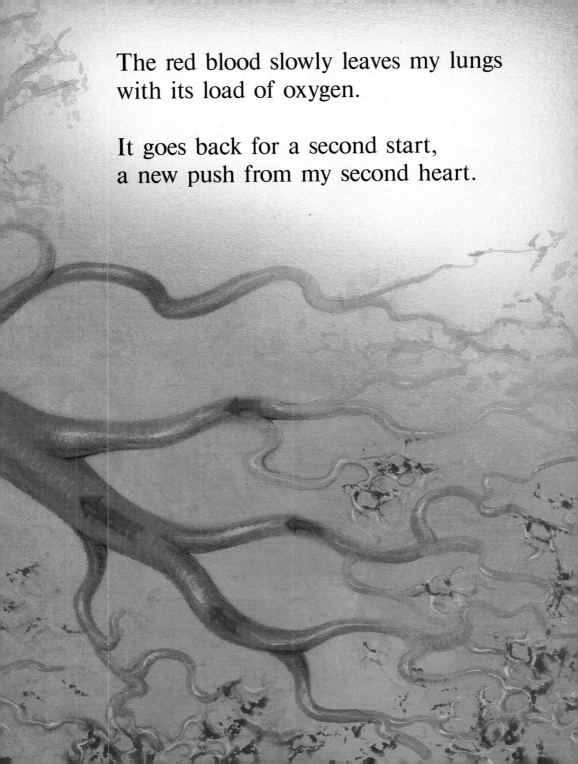

The red blood slowly leaves my lungs
with its load of oxygen.

It goes back for a second start,
a new push from my second heart.

So now my left heart
    fills with blood.
Again, a valve goes
    quickly shut.

Again,
    strong muscle-walls contract
with hearty force,
    blood rushes out.

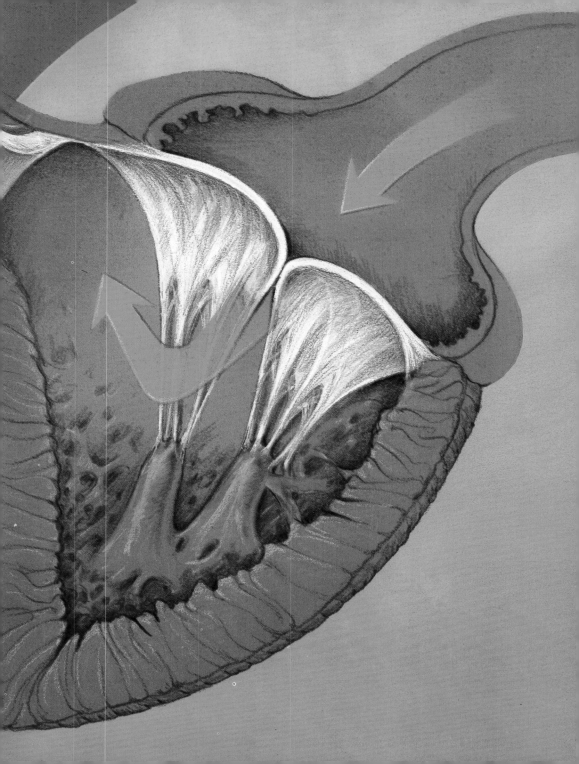

Now, bright red blood
with greatest speed
takes oxygen to every
part of me.

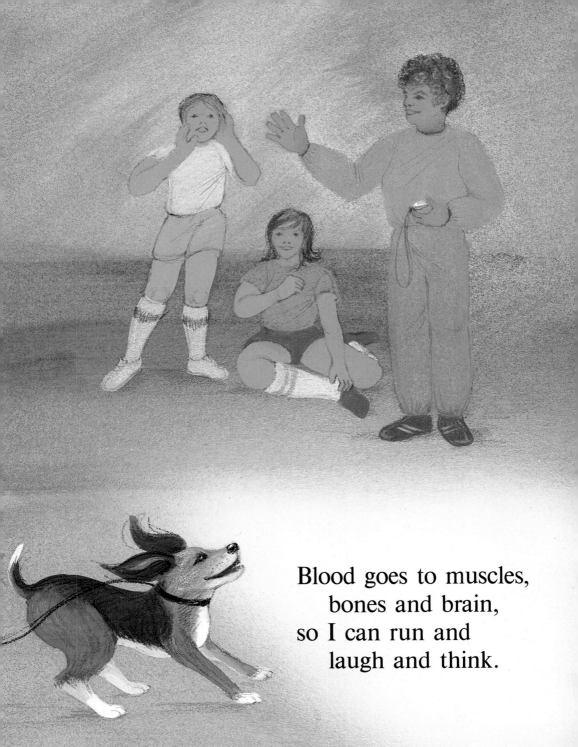

Blood goes to muscles,
bones and brain,
so I can run and
laugh and think.

I have two hearts that beat as one.

My right heart
pumps blood
to my lungs

My left heart
pumps to all
the rest.

Together,
    my two hearts work best!